The Beat of a Different Drummer

Not-So-Traditional Rudimental Solos for the Advanced Drummer

Dominick Cuccia

Published by
Meredith Music Publications
a division of G.W. Music, Inc.
4899 Lerch Creek Ct., Galesville, MD 20765
http://www.meredithmusic.com

MEREDITH MUSIC PUBLICATIONS and its stylized double M logo are trademarks of MEREDITH MUSIC PUBLICATIONS, a division of G.W. Music, Inc.

No part of this book may be reproduced or transmitted in any form or by any means, electronic or mechanical, including photocopying, recording, or by any informational storage or retrieval system without permission in writing from the publisher.

Copyright © 2004 MEREDITH MUSIC PUBLICATIONS
International Copyright Secured · All Rights Reserved
First Edition
April 2004

International Standard Book Number: 1-57463-032-6
Printed and bound in U.S.A.

This book is dedicated to:

My wife Therese, daughter Grace, and son Dominick! (All the inspiration I need!!!!!)

AND

My parents, Gaspare and Debbie Cuccia (Gus and Debbie); my brothers and sisters, Catherine Cavallo, Gus Cuccia Jr., Deborah Malli, Nicholas Cuccia, and Joseph Cuccia; and Bill Dillon, the "Tom Hagen" of the Family (see "The Godfather"). ALA FAMIGLIA!

and thanks to the Masters

Thomas Cecil Andrews, Frank Arsenault, Nick Attanasio, Dr. Berger, Dave Boddie, Bruce and Emmett, Paul Cormier, Bobby Culkin, Jeff Funnell, Harold Green, Ed Lemley, Ken Lemley, Mitch Markowich, Gus Moeller, J. Burns Moore, Joe Morello, Les Parks, Charley Poole Jr., Jack Pratt, Hugh Quigley, Bob Redican, George Lawrence Stone, Earl Sturtze, Al "Duke" Terreri, Bobby Thompson, and Bill Westphal.

AND

The Young Colonials, O.H. Booth Hose, The Civil War Troopers and The Regulators!

AND

Alan Cavallo; Traci, Maria, and Elizabeth Cuccia; Jason, Ian, Catherine, Sophia, and Jason Mathew Malli; Tracey and Shannon Cuccia; Kristine and Mathew Cuccia; Marylou and Whitney Rock; Joe, Lucille, and all the little Rocks—Joseph, James, Rachael, Johnathan, Jacob, and Rebecca; and everyone at The Daily Bloomer!

Table of Contents

Introduction iv
Rudiment Interpretation 1
Under The Influence 4
The Lonesome Scot & The Rocky Road To Dublin 7
On The Verge Of Tradition 8
Black Magic 10
Spur Of The Moment (bass solo) 12
Moments Later (bass solo) 14
Rhumba For Gus 17
Sammy & Dickerson 20
The Barrett Hill Project 22
Hidden Passage 25
Salamanca 28
Juh Dut Jut Jat 31
The Hellcats! 34
Hang Five 36
The Next Generation 39
My Friend Jack 42
About the Composer 44

Introduction

"If a man does not keep pace with his companions, perhaps it is because he hears a different drummer. Let him step to the music he hears, however measured or far away."

—Thoreau, "Conclusion," *Walden* (1854)

In life, there are times when we hear or read certain words and they describe our beliefs perfectly. This book contains "traditional" style rudimental drum solos in "not so traditional" settings. You might say it is a diary of my drumming life.

Each solo was inspired by people I admire, idolize, have drummed with, or dream of performing with some day. I have been lucky to be around some outstanding musicians and have had teaching and performing opportunities I could only have dreamed of as a child!

Although I was brought up in a traditional rudimental drumming environment, I am far from a traditionalist. In this book you will not find much music you can play as you march down the street. Instead, you will discover a combination of traditional and contemporary techniques, intertwined to create unique musical solos.

As you play these selections, you will notice every sticking is included so there will be no speculation as to how a figure is played. With that said, I believe this style of drumming is definitely in the vein of jazz. Unlike a lot of contemporary drumming, where every note is written out with no room for interpretation or imagination, the use of grace notes on flam, drag, and ratamacue figures give the performer the opportunity to create something unique. I have included an interpretation page that displays how I would play the grace note figures (usually!); this doesn't mean you must perform it this way.

The best way to use this book is to learn each solo as written and practice with a metronome. Try to play them utilizing the Rudiment Interpretation, pages 1–3. These solos were usually played between 104 and 112 beats per minutes. Once you've mastered them within these parameters, make them your own. Do not stick to the tempos if they stifle your creativity.

I have experimented with playing them as slow as 80 beats per minute and as fast as 120, and in some cases they actually groove better at alternative tempos. You will also notice that I have utilized the method of notation (beaming across the bar line) made popular by John S. Pratt. Using these extended beams should help you identify rudiments as you approach them.

I hope you enjoy performing and listening to these solos. They truly have provided a lifetime of enjoyment for me and I hope they will not only inspire you to play, but create as well.

In order to be successful in music, we must all try to become "different drummers." We must utilize the power of the imagination, and "step to the music we hear."

Rudiment Interpretation

This is a basic explanation of how the rudiments are to be interpreted. Please do not consider these the rules for all rudimental drumming. Some people may have different ideas, this is just how I believe the rudiments should be played in certain situations. A quick note about rolls. I've been asked "if a 7 stroke roll is based on a triplet, why don't we just eliminate the 7 and replace it with a 3?" My answer is the triplet is implied and although 3 may be "theoretically" correct, the tradition is to put the 7 above the roll. This goes for all rolls. Some have a quintuplet or septuplet base, but it is implied and the actual roll number is displayed. Also, accents have been put on traditional beats, but are not always played that way in the solos.

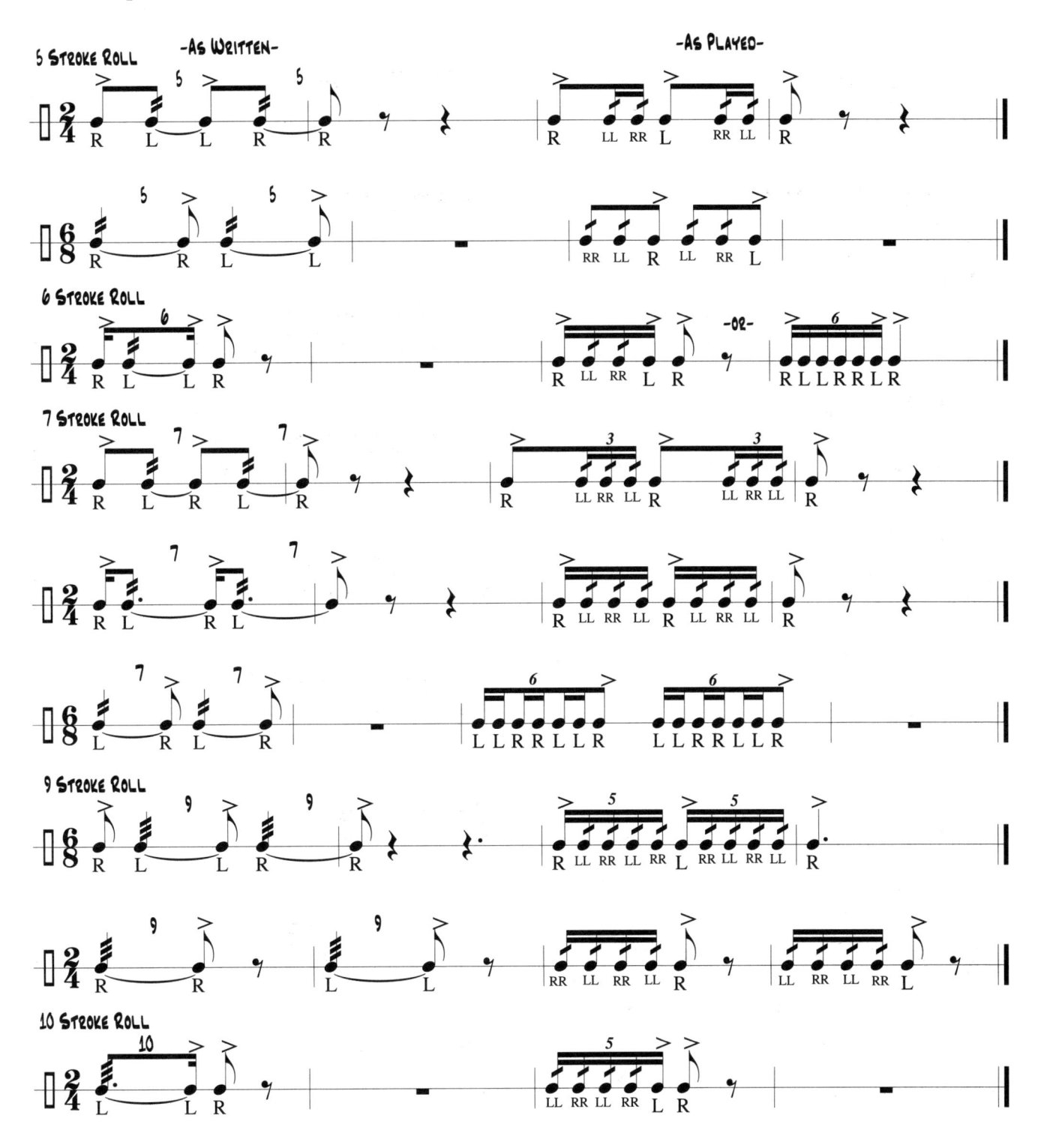

11 Stroke Roll

13 Stroke Roll

15 Stroke Roll

Ruff or Half Drag

(off tap)

-As Written-
-As Played-
Lesson 25
Drag Paradiddle #1
Drag Paradiddle #2
Single Drag
Double Drag
-or-
Single Ratamacue
Double Ratamacue
Triple Ratamacue

Under The Influence (1985)

As a beginning drummer I was very lucky to have two motivational instructors, Gary Gilloti and Mary Comer (now Mary Saunders). They were both brought up in the Earl Sturtze school of drumming and "Under Their Influence" I've been able to spend my life living and loving rudimental drumming! My first attempts at composing for solo snare drum were influenced by many of the great "contemporary ancients." Although they may not have known it, Paul Cormier, Bobby Culkin, Javier Morales, Les Parks, Charley Poole, Jr., John S. Pratt, Al "Duke" Terreri, Bobby Thompson, and Bill Westphal have all inspired me immeasurably. This solo is dedicated to all of these influential individuals!

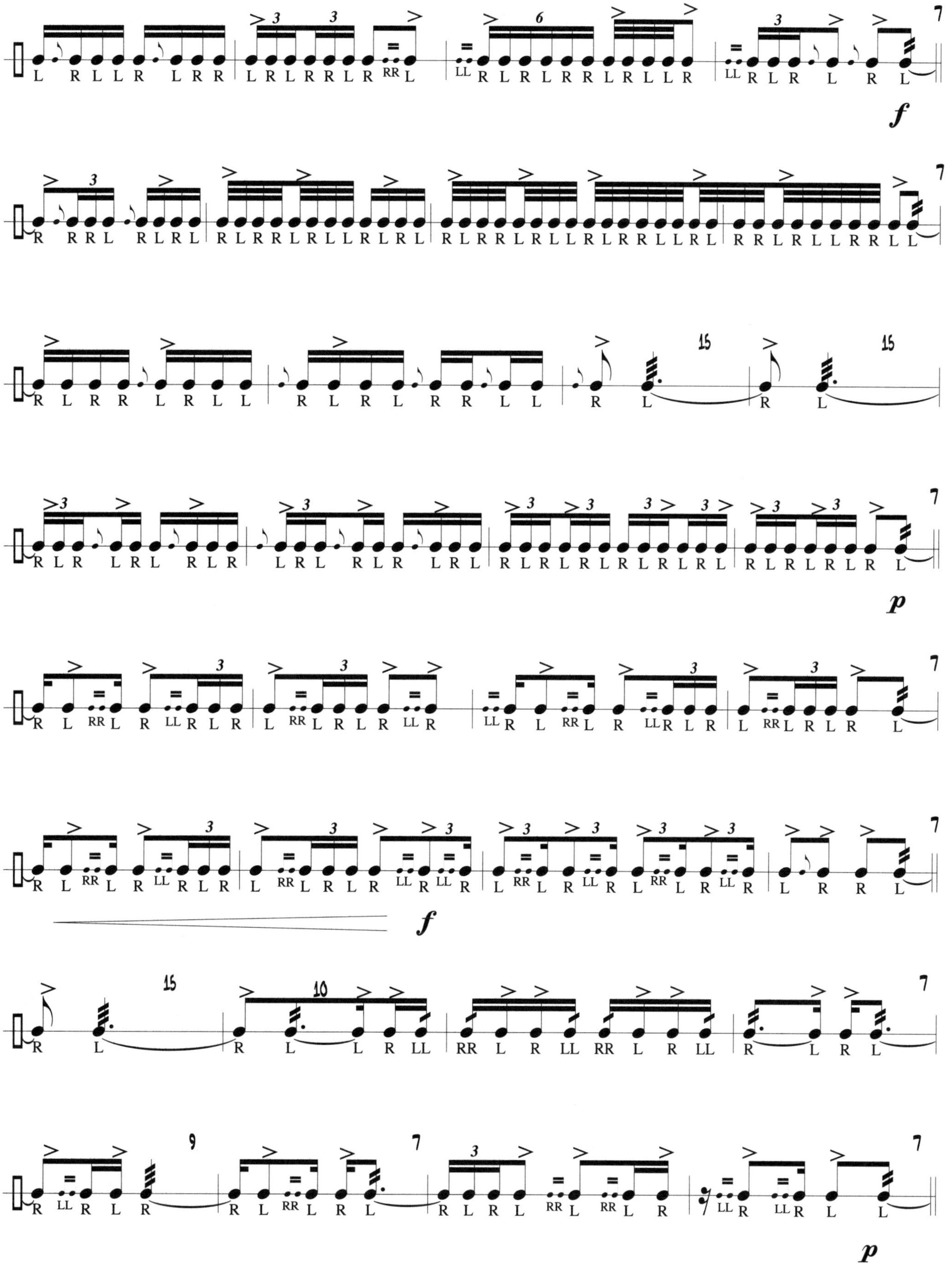

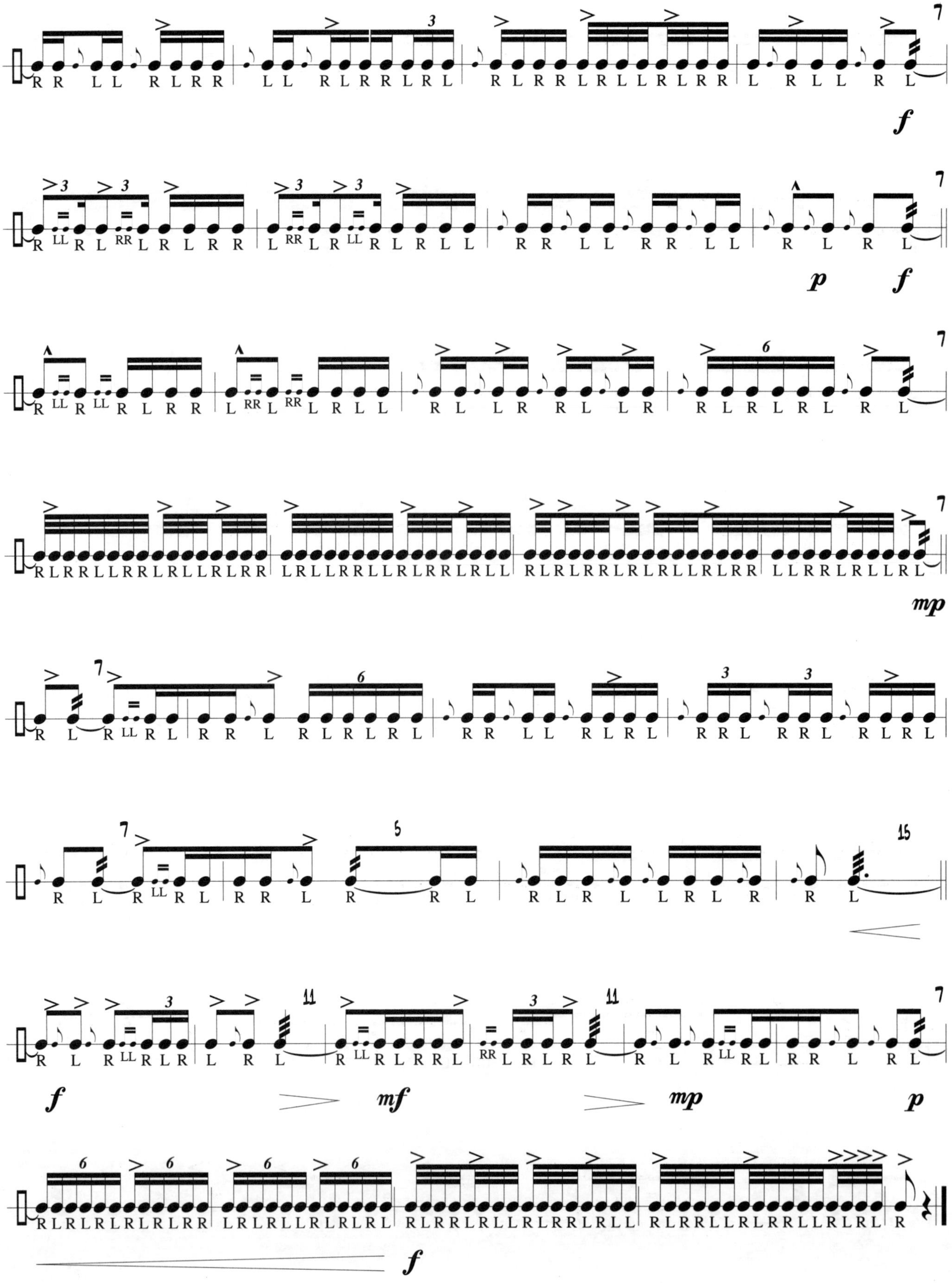

The Lonesome Scot & The Rocky Road to Dublin (1991/2002)

I wrote *The Lonesome Scot* when I was stationed at West Point following a lesson with Joe Morello. It was a favorite song of mine and I had a creative burst that led to the drum part. However, the part never caught on and I only played it a handful of times. Eleven years later at the Young Colonials 15th Annual Muster I found myself surprisingly playing it in a late night jam session with the only other drummer who might possibly know it by my side, my brother, Gus. I felt compelled to add it to the book but I knew I would need another good slip jig (a jig in 9/8). *Rocky Road to Dublin* was the first tune that came to my mind and I wrote the part specifically for this book.

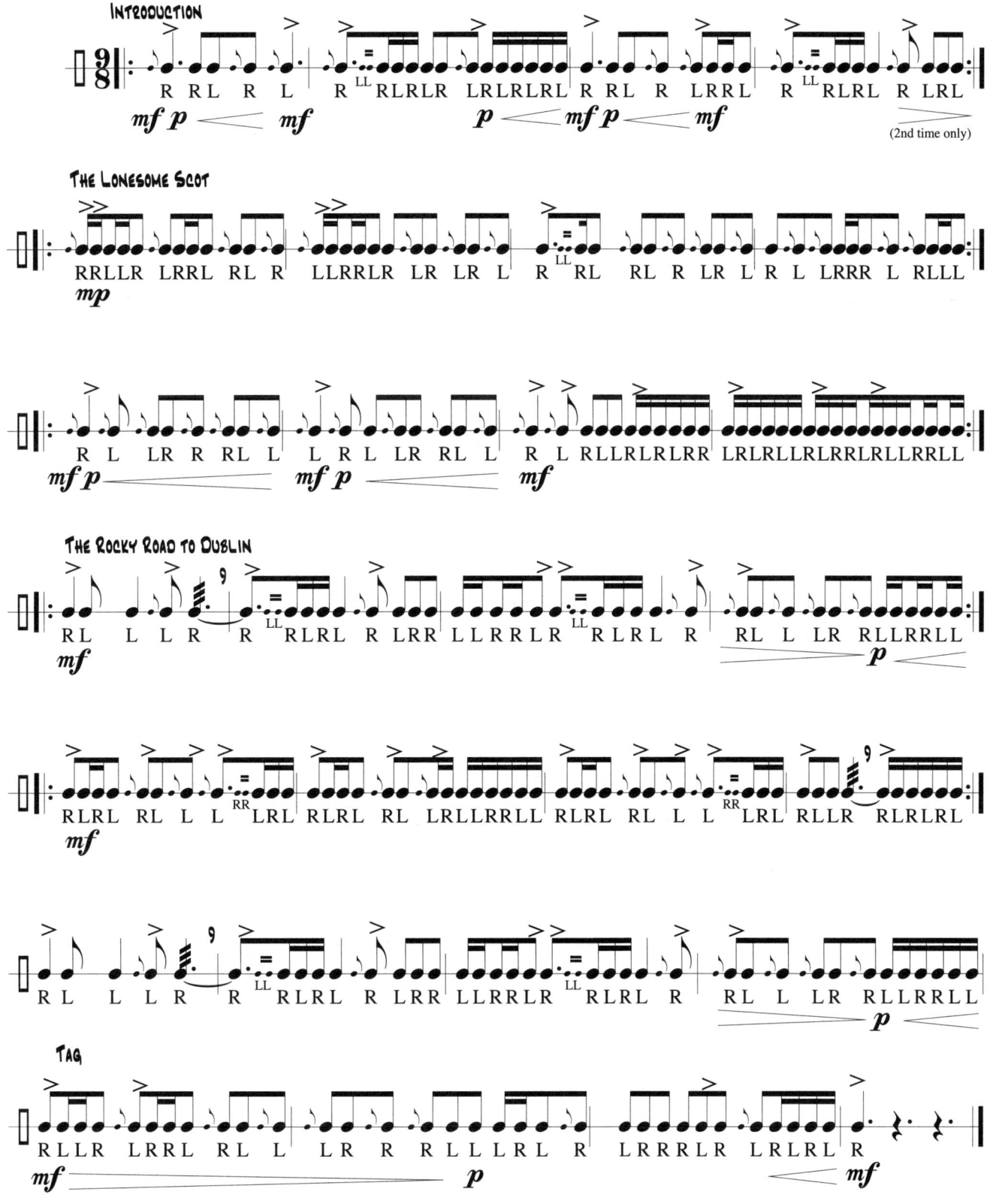

On the Verge of Tradition (1987)

In the fall of 1985 I entered Wilkes College in Wilkes-Barre, Pennsylvania as a music education major. The percussion instructor was Bob Nowak and although he had me focus on concert and world percussion, he always encouraged me to continue with my true love, rudimental drumming.

I wrote this solo in the fall of my junior year and dedicate it to Bob.

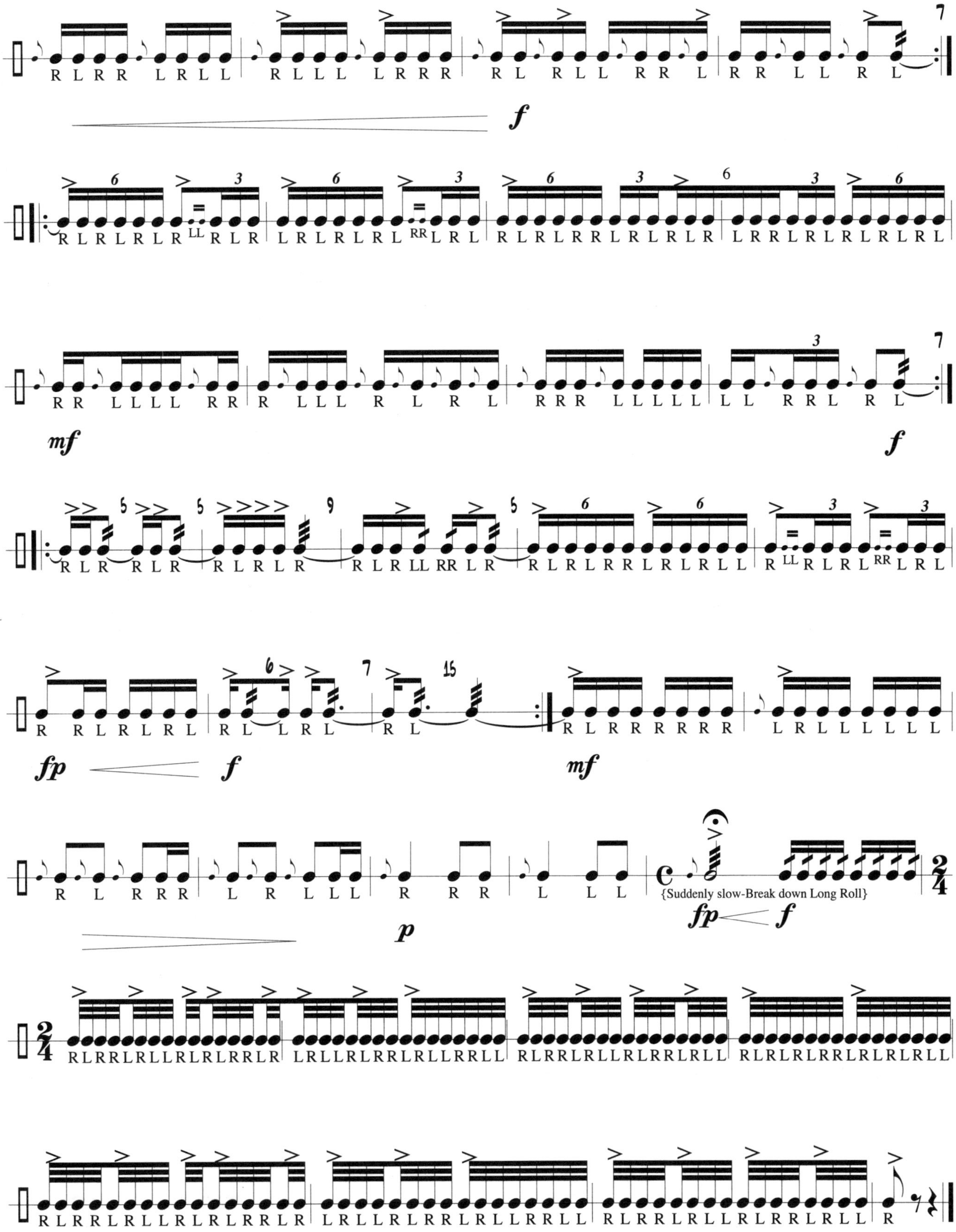
{Suddenly slow-Break down Long Roll}
f
mf
fp
p

Black Magic (1988)

Two major musical influences in my life have been Steve Fidyk and Steve Primatic. We met as students at Wilkes University and they have gone on to have wonderful careers in the world of drums and percussion. Primatic is a member of the faculty at Armstrong Atlantic State University in Savannah, Georgia, teaching percussion, theory and jazz. Fidyk is the drummer with the US Army Blues in Washington D.C. as well as director of drumset studies at the University of Maryland and adjunct professor at George Mason University. Both of these guys are not only top musicians, but also world class people. I believe I not only benefitted musically from drumming with them, but socially from their friendship as well.

(29-32, X=backstick)
(33-38, X=stick click)
1.Put right stick under left arm.
2. Left stick goes into right & is played as backstick.
3. Left hand plays with stick that was under arm.
4. Right stick does half flip & plays rim shot.
(43-end, X=rim shot)
accel.
accel.

Spur of the Moment (Bass Drum Solo) (1988)

The late 1980s saw my brother Nicholas rapidly becoming one of the top junior bass drummers in the world of fifing & drumming. To help achieve his goals he decided to study with the master of rudimental bass drum, Nick Attanasio. Under his tutelage, he went on to win 4 consecutive individual bass drum titles at the Northeastern Championships. I attended all of their drum lessons and learned a lot just by listening. At the 1988 contest I was defending my bass title and actually lost to my brother. It was a loss I do not regret. This was the first time I improvised on the individual stand and it produced this solo, which I dedicate to both Nicholas and Nick (the student and the master).

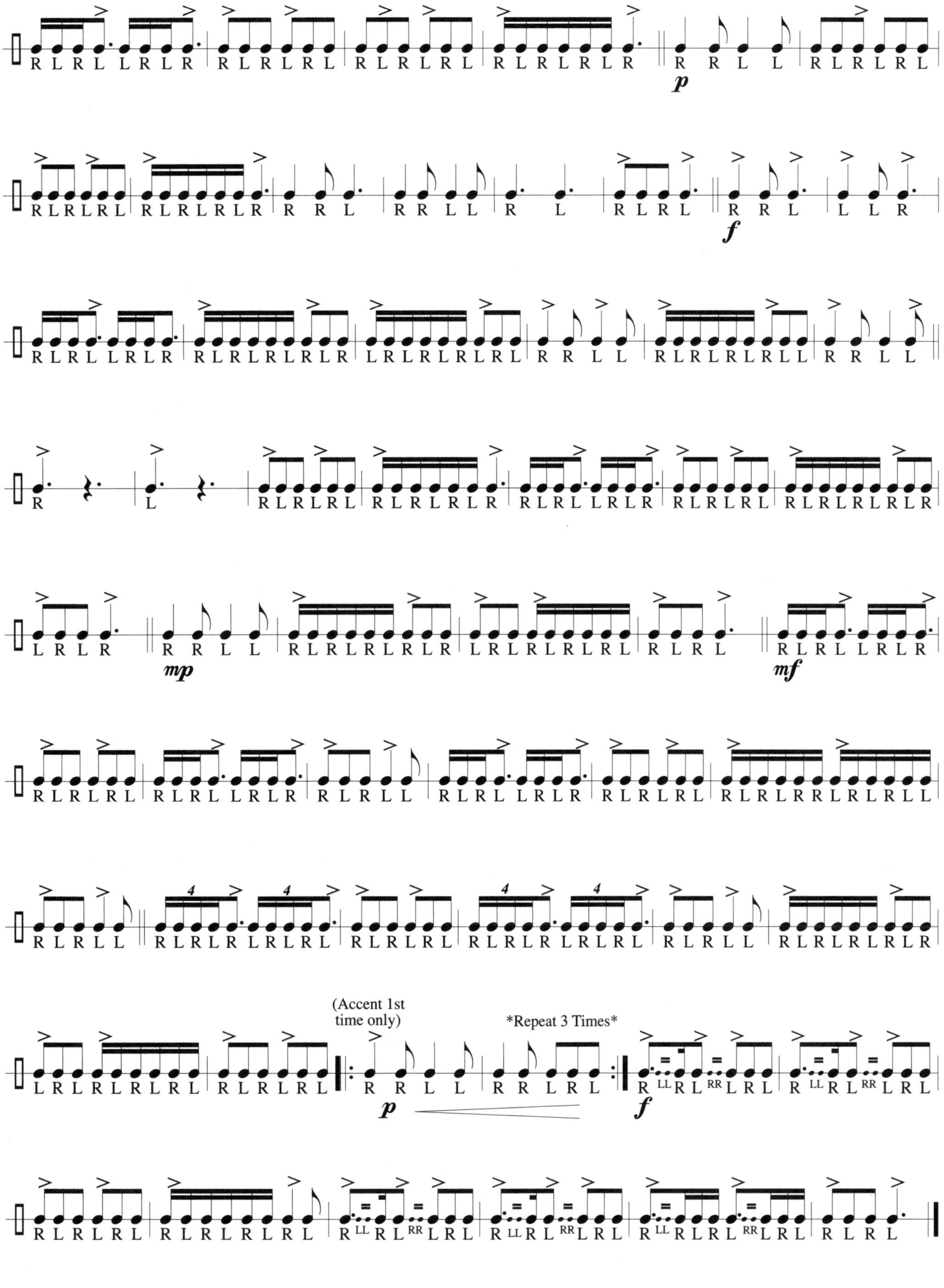
(Accent 1st time only)
Repeat 3 Times

Moments Later (Bass Drum Solo) (1988)

The Northeastern Championship is the biggest title available for a competitive fife and drum corp. As a soloist you must perform two selections, one in 2/4, the other in 6/8. Here is my improvised 2/4 selection which I'd like to dedicate to my mom and dad. They are two truly inspirational people, the reason I'm a drummer today. It was their idea for me to join a band. Dad retired from his job with the NYC Subway in the early 1990s and in 1994 decided to learn the bass drum. Together they are the heart and soul of The Regulators Fife & Drum Corps, with dad the anchor of the bass line and mom the color guard captain. Although this solo was created years before they started marching, it would never have become a reality without them.

15

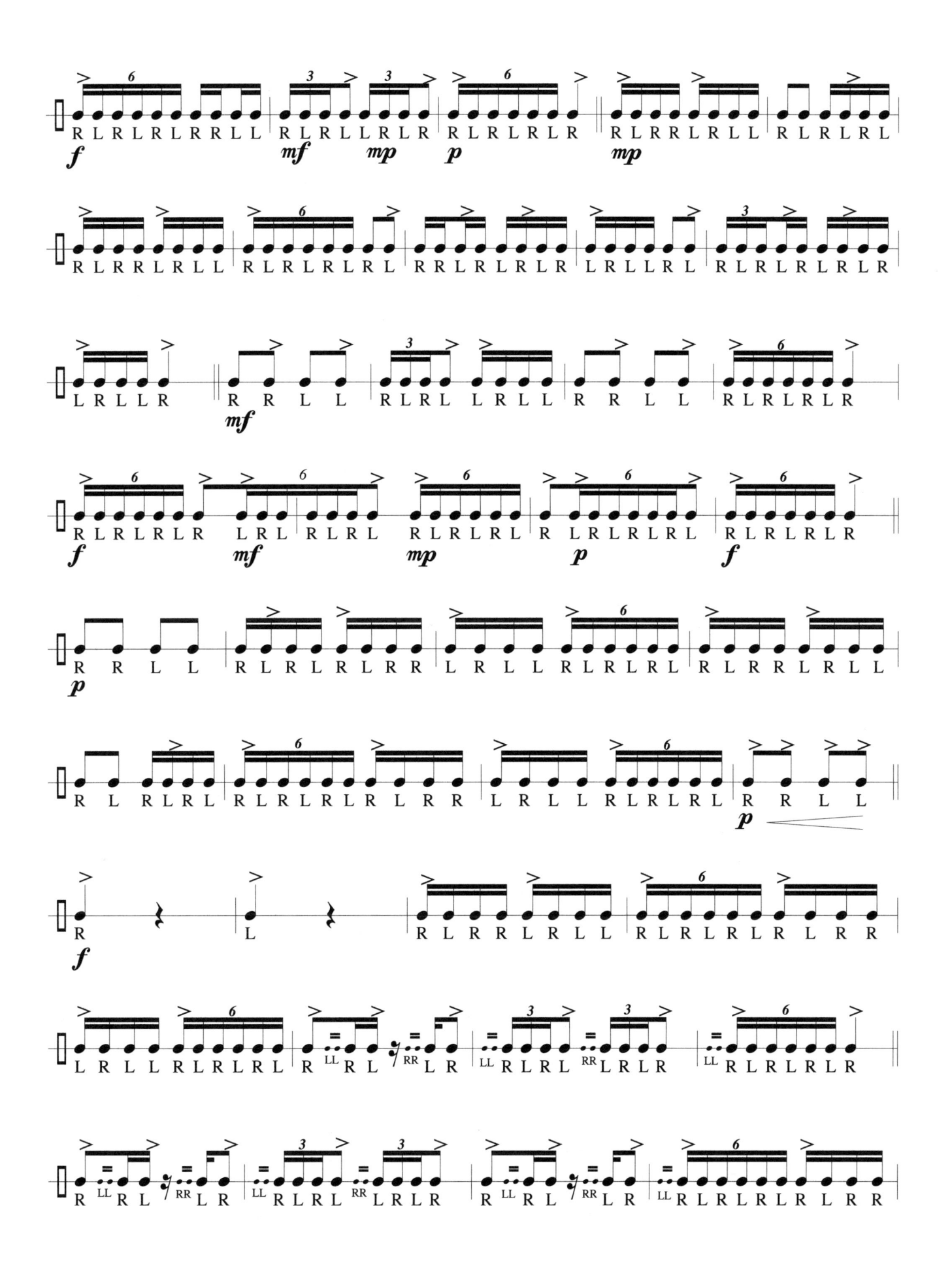

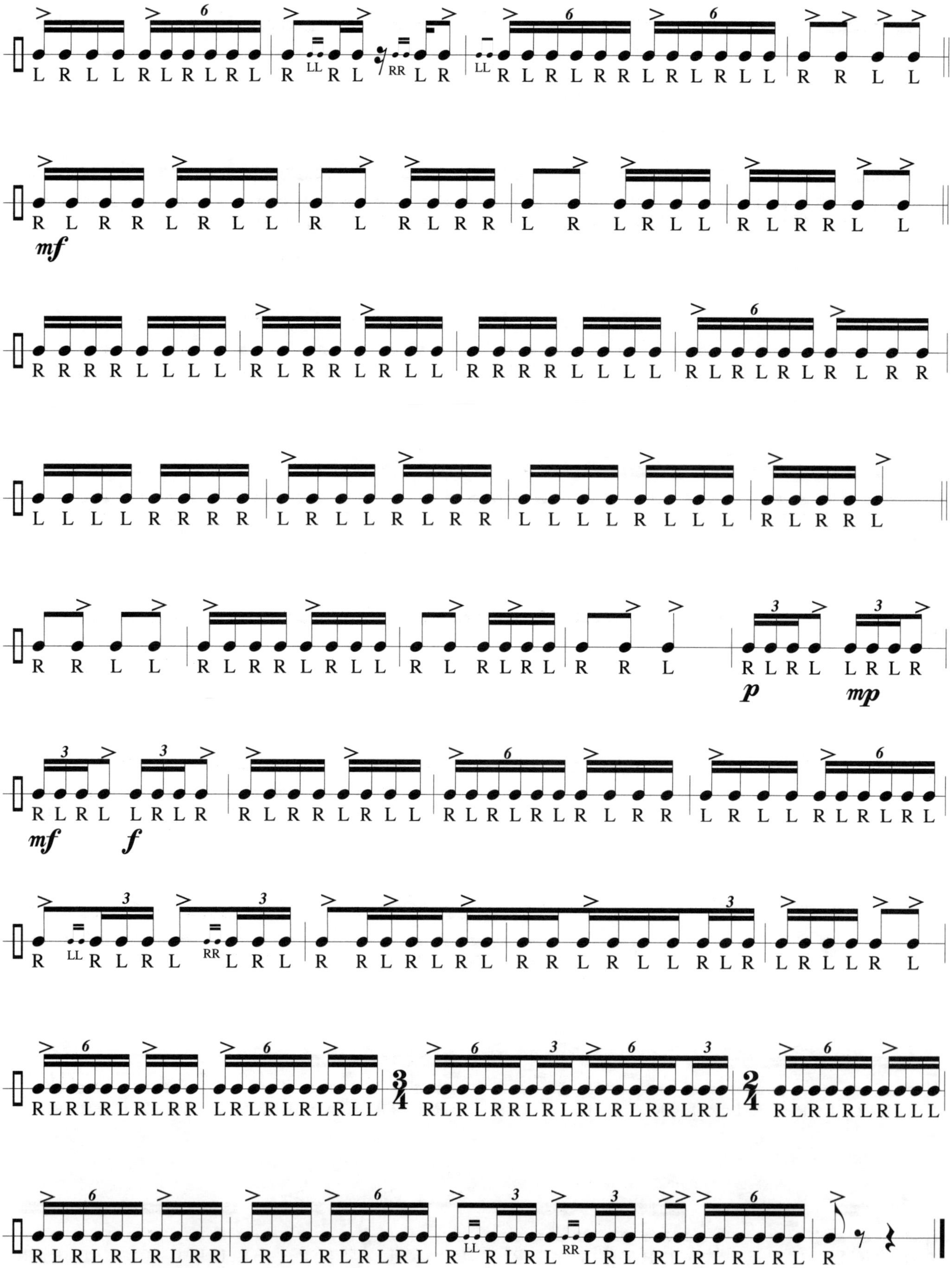
L R L L R L R L R L R LL R L RR L R LL R L R L R R L R L R L L R R L L
R L R R L R L L R L R L R R L R L R L L R L R R L L
mf
R R R R L L L L R L R R L R L L R R R R L L L L R L R L R L R L R R
L L L L R R R R L R L L R L R R L L L L R L L L R L R R L
R R L L R L R R L R L L R L R L R L R R L R L R L L R L R
p
mp
R L R L L R L R R L R R L R L L R L R L R L R L R R L R L L R L R L R L
mf
f
R LL R L R L RR L R L R R L R L R L R R L R L L R L R L R L L R L
RLRLRLRLRR LRLRLRLRLL RLRLRRLRLRLRLRRLRL RLRLRLRLLL
RLRLRLRLRR LRLLRLRLRL R LL RLRL RR LRL RLRLRLRL R

Rhumba For Gus (1989)

In the late '80s there was a new force emerging among junior ancient snare drummers—my brother Gus Cuccia, Jr. After having success with solos written for other people, he wanted something of his own to set him apart from his competitors. This solo definitely has personality. In 1990, Gus and his Rhumba were undefeated, winning every major championship, and presenting a memorable performance at the DCI solo and ensemble contest. (Note: he was playing on his rope drum!) Many of my solos have either been premiered by or written for Gus. In some cases I think he is the only one who can play them. I must tell you that his drumming and musical mind have been a constant source of inspiration for me and I believe he is truly one of the great rudimental drummers of our time.

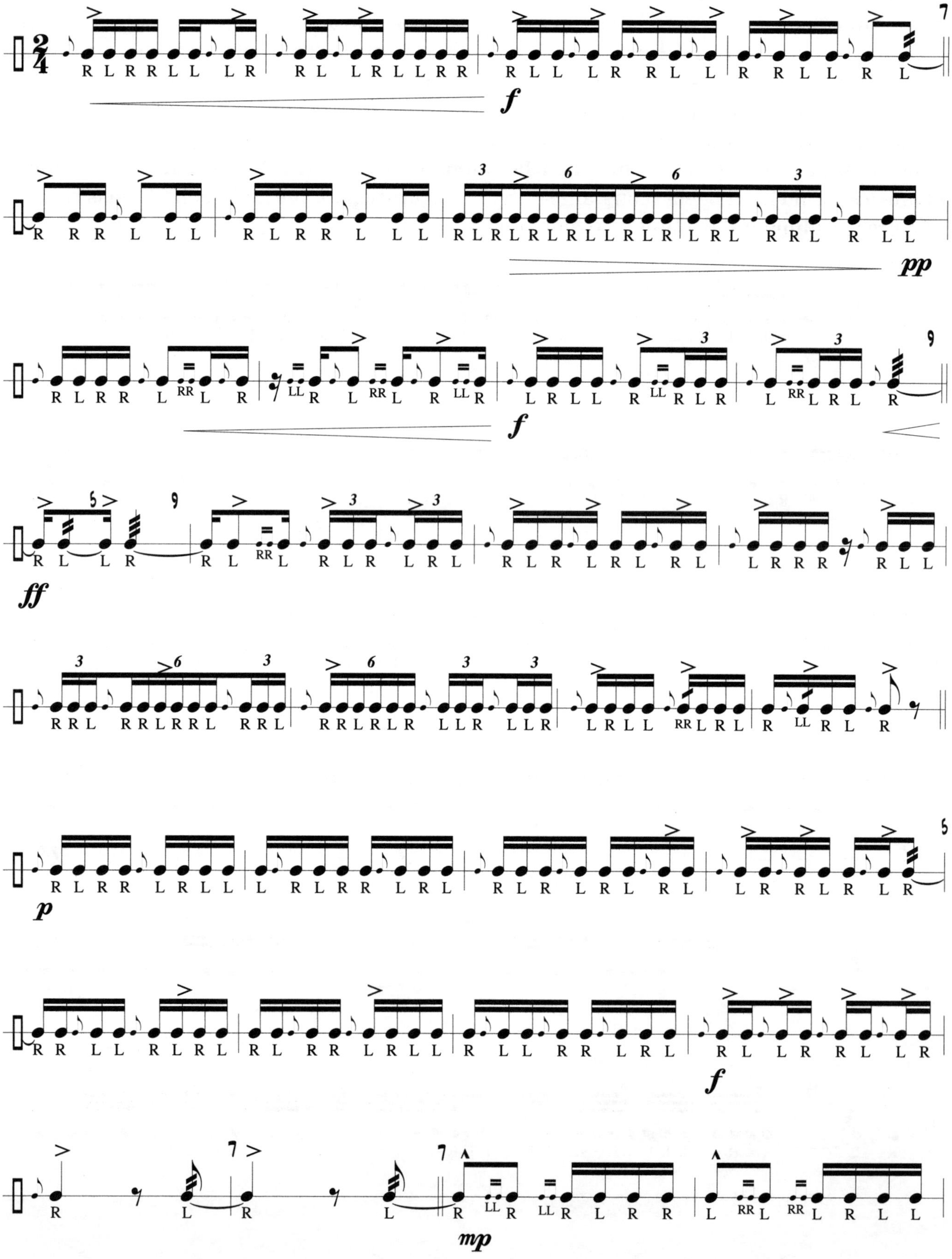
f
pp
f
ff
p
f
mp

19

Sammy & Dickerson (1989/2002)

One of the classiest and most unique groups in the fife & drum world is the Charles W. Dickerson Field Music from New Rochelle, New York. During the early '80s I became friends with Sammy Romie, a snare drummer with the corps. He was taught by "the master," Dave Boddie, who was taught by the legendary Sanford A. "Gus" Moeller. Mr. Moeller was the man who defined the "Dickerson style." If you've ever wondered what it means to look natural while you play, you only have to look as far as Dickerson. When I was a kid, Sammy always shared his knowledge through stories, example and performance, and I am forever grateful. This solo also contains stickings I learned by playing the music of Cecil Andrews, a member since 1938. *Sammy* was written in 1989 for the Young Colonials album *Friendship Through Music* while *Dickerson* was written in 2002 as a tribute to Dave, Gus, Cecil, and Dickerson.

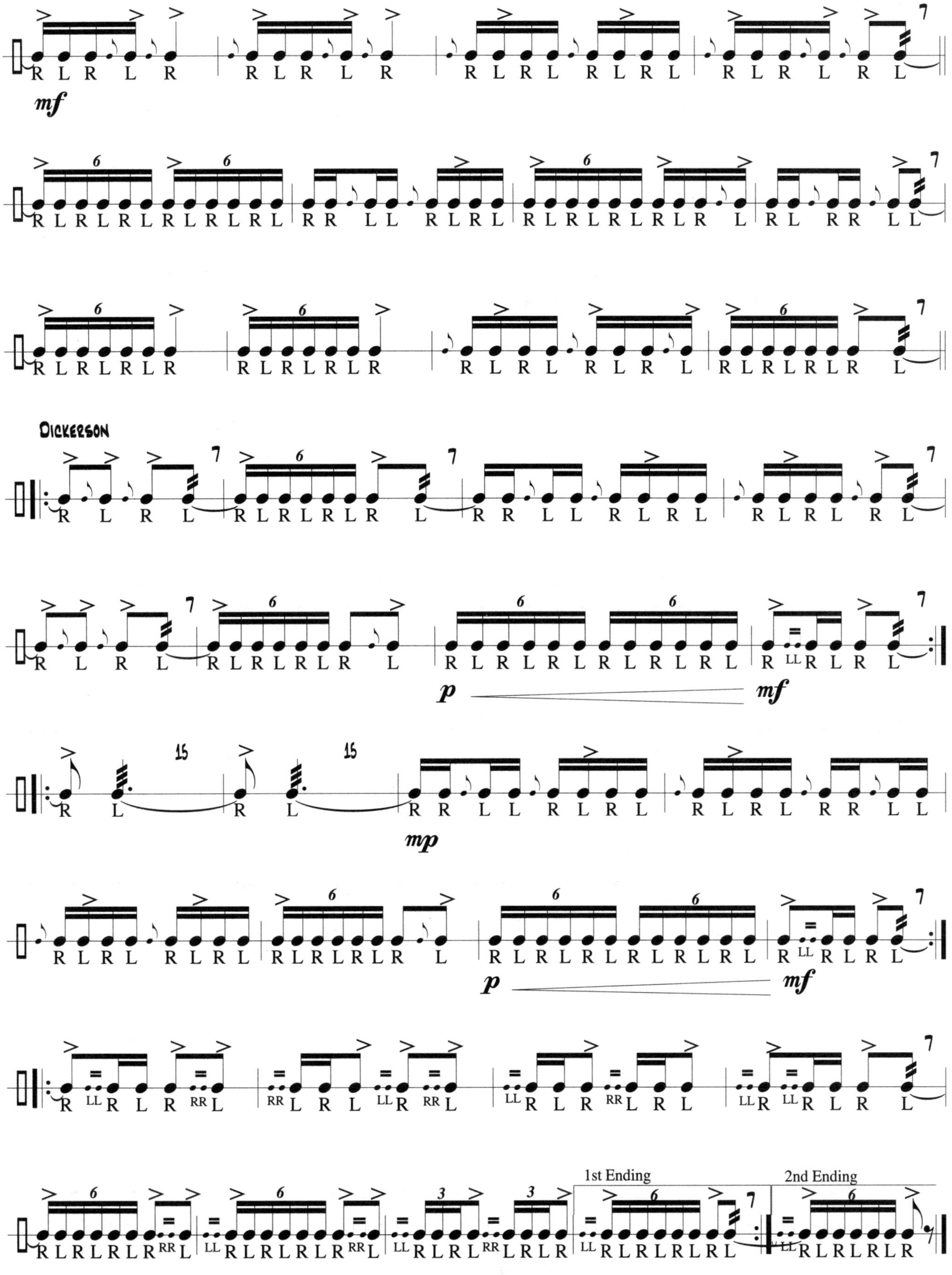
mf
Dickerson
p
mf
mp
p
mf
1st Ending
2nd Ending

The Barrett Hill Project (1990)

During my tenure teaching the Young Colonials Fife & Drum Corps, all of our drummers were very successful in solo competition. Bill Dillon, with the corps since 1980, asked me to write him a solo. As it turned out this is one of my favorites to listen to, as well as play. Bill did an outstanding job with it, ending the 1990 season as one of the top finalists at the Northeastern Championships. After leaving the Young Colonials, Bill went on to perform with a number of drum and bugle corps including the Rochester Patriots, Connecticut Hurricanes and the Bushwackers, as well as to instruct the legendary Danbury Drum Corps. It's interesting to note that the title comes from the road Bill lived on as a kid.

R L R L R L R R L L R L L R R L R L R L L R R L R L R LL R L L
f p
R L R L R L R L R L R L R L R L R L R L R L R L R L R L R L L
mf f
R L R R L R L R L R L R L L R L R LL R L RR L RR L R LL R L R L R L R L R LL R L
RR L RR L R L R L R L R R L R L R L L R L R L R L R L R L R L R L R L R
R L R L R L R L R L R L L R L R R L R L L R L R
L R L R L R L R L R L R L R L R L R L R L R L
p
R L R L R L R L R L R L R L R L R L R L R LL R L RR L RR L R LL R L L
R L R L R L R L R L R L R L R R L L R L R L R L R L L R L R L R L R R
f
L R L R L R R L L R L R L L R L R L R LL R L RR L R L R L R L R

R L R L R L R L R L R L R R L L R L R L R L R LL R L L
p
R L R L R L R R L L R L L R R L R L R L L R R L R L R LL R L L
f
p
R L R L R L R L R L R L R L R L R L R L R L R L R L R L L
mf
f
R L R R L R L R L R L R L L R L R LL R L RR L RR L R LL R L R L R L R LL R L
RR L RR L R L R L R L R L R R L R L R L L R L R L R L R L R L R L R L
R L R L R L R L R L R L R L RR L R LL R L R L R L R L R L R L R L R
p
f
3
R L R L R L R L R L R L L RR L R LL R L R L R L R L R L R L R LL R L RR L R R

Hidden Passage (1990)

I have always been a fan of drumming legend Joe Morello and have been fortunate enough to take a few lessons with him. You will probably notice in this solo some 'Morello-esque' licks. Thanks for the music, Joe. Writing this solo was easy and difficult at the same time. I wrote the first 16 bars rather easily, but found myself stumped figuring what would come next. I decided to write another 16 bar theme and base the rest of the solo on these rhythmical developments. After a gradual increase in technical demand the solo has a recapitulation of the first 8 bars. Then, with the '87 Cadets and '88 Blue Devils in mind, the final 8 bars summarize each variation, and fade out into a statement of the initial theme.

L R L R L R L L R R L R L R R L R L R L L R L R L R
p
L R L L R L R L R L R L R L R L R L R R L RR L RR L R L L R L R L R L R L
f
p
RR L R L R L R L R L R L R L R L R LL R L R R L RR L R L L R LL R L R LL R L R LL R L
f
p
f
R R L RR L L R LL R L R LL R L R L R L R L L R LL R L R R L R L L R LL R L R L R
R LLRR L RR L RRLL R R R L L R R L L R R L L R LLRR L R L RRLL R R L L R R L L
R L R L L L R L R R R R L L L L L L L R R R R R R R R R
p
L L R L L L L R L R L R L L L L R L R R L L R L R L RLRL
f
p
R L R L R L R R L L L R L R R R R L L L L L L L L R R R R
f
R L L L L R LLRR L R L RRLL R L R L R LRLR L L RLR L L L L L
p

27

Salamanca (1991)

During the 1990s the Young Colonials sent many drummers into the professional ranks. Therese Rock began playing with the corps in 1987. When I vacated the instructor's position in 1994, she stepped right in and in 1995, her drumline led the corps to a victory at the Northeastern Championships. The following year she relocated to Orlando, Florida to perform with The Spirit of America (formerly The Sons of Liberty) fife & drum corps at Walt Disney World's EPCOT Center. Therese was the first woman to be accepted into the group, and management thought the original name wouldn't be appropriate (thus the name change.) The title of this solo comes from the University of Salamanca in Spain where she was studying when it was written.

R L R L L R R L R L R L R L R R L L R L R L R L R L R R L L
L R L L R R R L R L R L R R LL R LL R L R L RR L RR L R LL R L
f
R R L RR L R LL R L R L L R L R L R L R L R L R L R L R L R L R L R L R L R L
R LL R L R L R L L R L R L R L L R L R L R L
mf
mp
p
R L R R R L R LL R LL R L R R L L R L R L R L R
f
p
L RR L RR L R L L R R L L R L R R L R L L R L R L R R L L R L R R
R L L R L R L R L R LL R R L RR L L R L RR L R L R L R L R R L RR L L R
f
LL R L RR L R L R L R LL R L R L RR L R L R L RR L R L R L R L R L R L RR L R L R
LL R L RR L R L L R R R R R R R
mp

L L L L L R L R L R L L R L R L R L R R L R R L L
mf p
R L R L R L R L R L R L R L R LL R L RR L RR L R L
fp fp
R L RR L RR L R LL R LL R LL R L R L RR L R L R LL R LL R L R L RR L R L R
f
LL R L R L R L R L R L R L R L R L R L R L R L R R L L
p
R L R L R L R R R L R L R R L R L R
f p
L L R L R L R L R L R R L L R L R L R R L R L R L R R L L R L
f
R L R L L R L R L R L L R R L R R L R L R L R L R R R L R L L R R L R
L R L R L R L R LL R L RR L R LL R L R L L R R L R L R L R L L L R L R R L R

Juh Dut Jut Jat (1995)

I believe drummers speak a language that most people don't understand. Because of this we're looked at many times as strange (in reality I think we like it that way!). *Juh Dut Jut Jat* is the main theme of this solo and if you use your imagination you'll be singing it long after you're done playing. At the time this solo was written I was working on my masters degree at Northwestern State University of Louisiana. Many drummers affected the writing of this solo although they may not have known it, so I'd like to dedicate this solo to the NSU drumline under the direction of my good friend and mentor, Ken Green, and director of bands, Bill Brent.

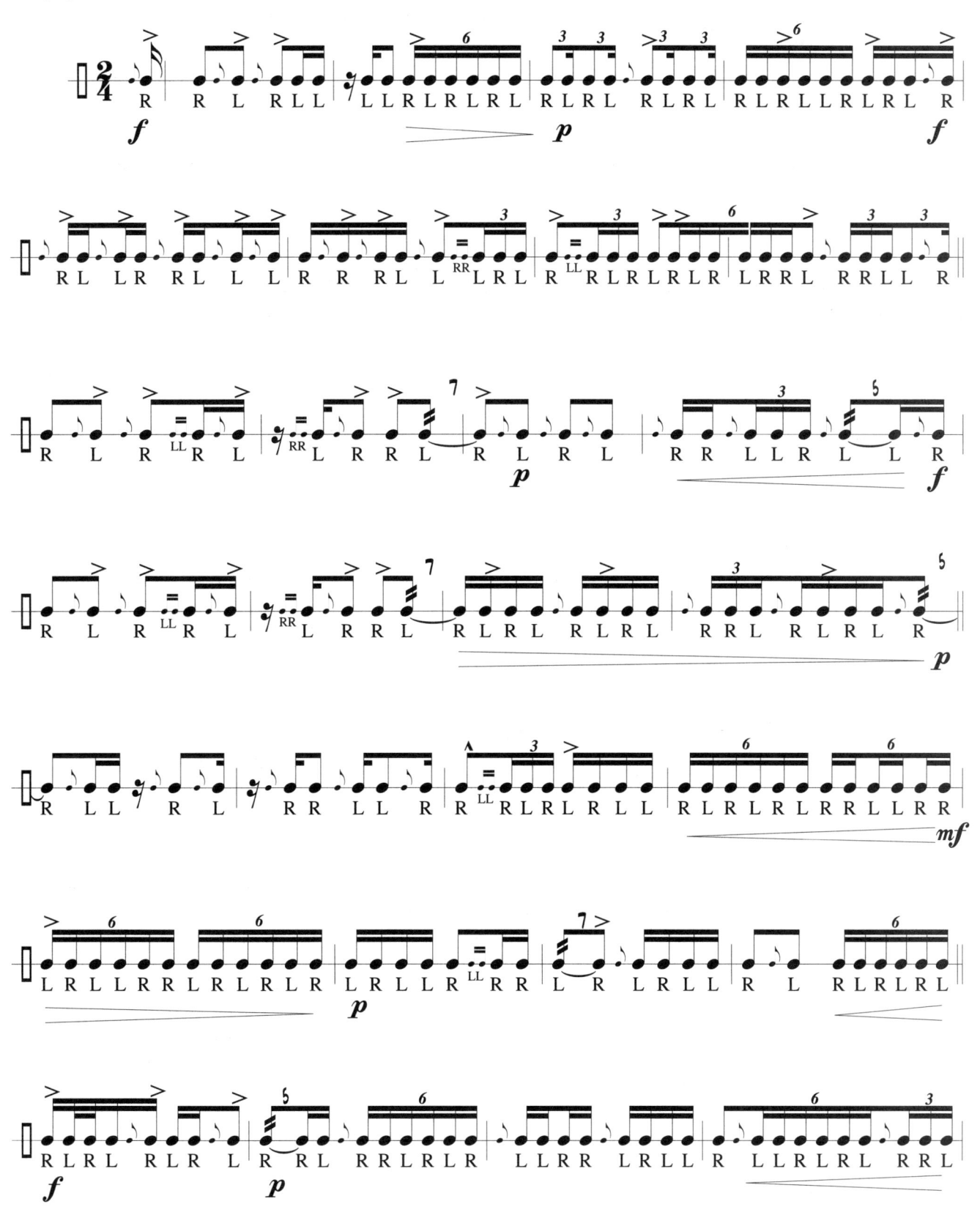

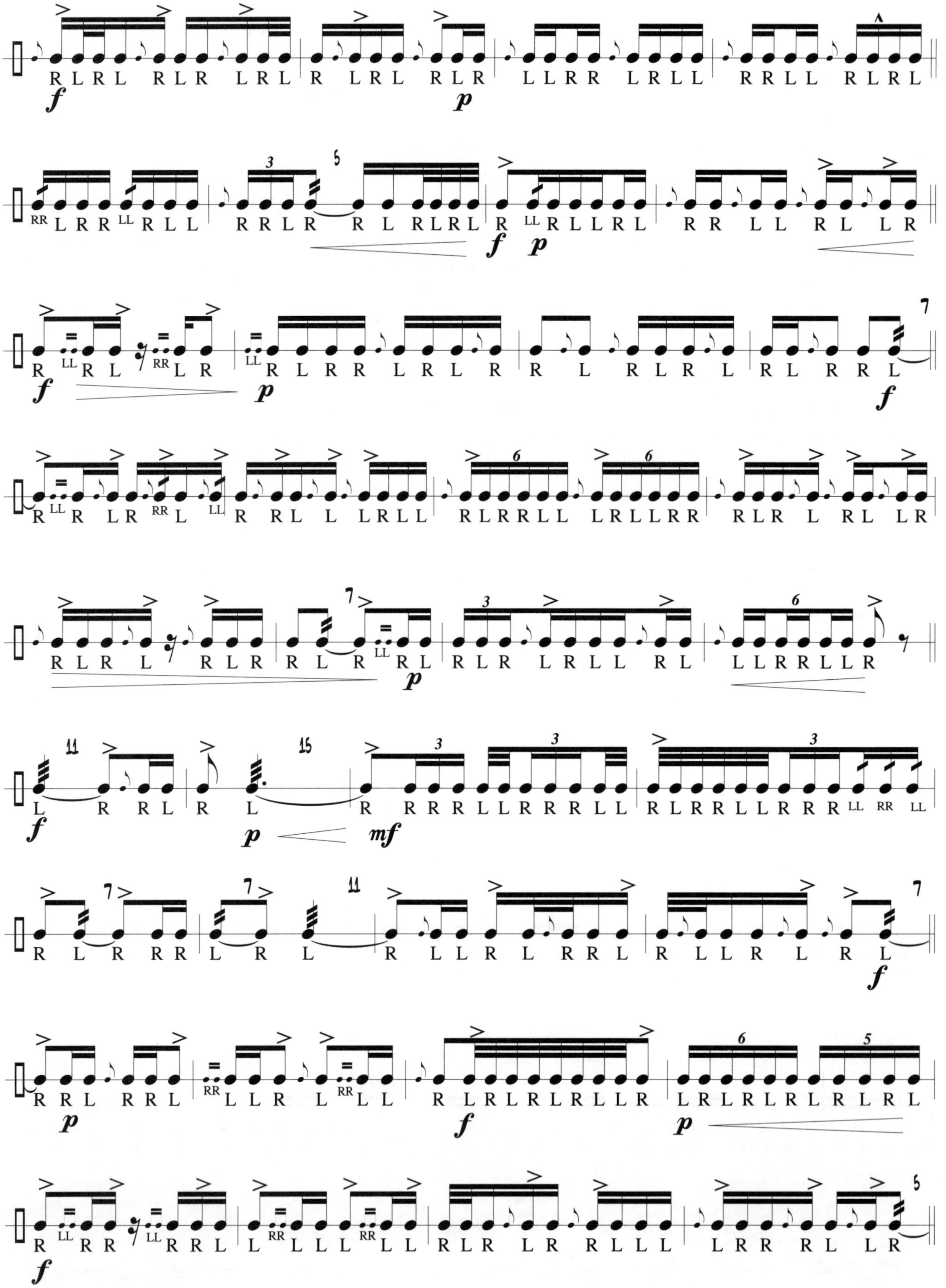

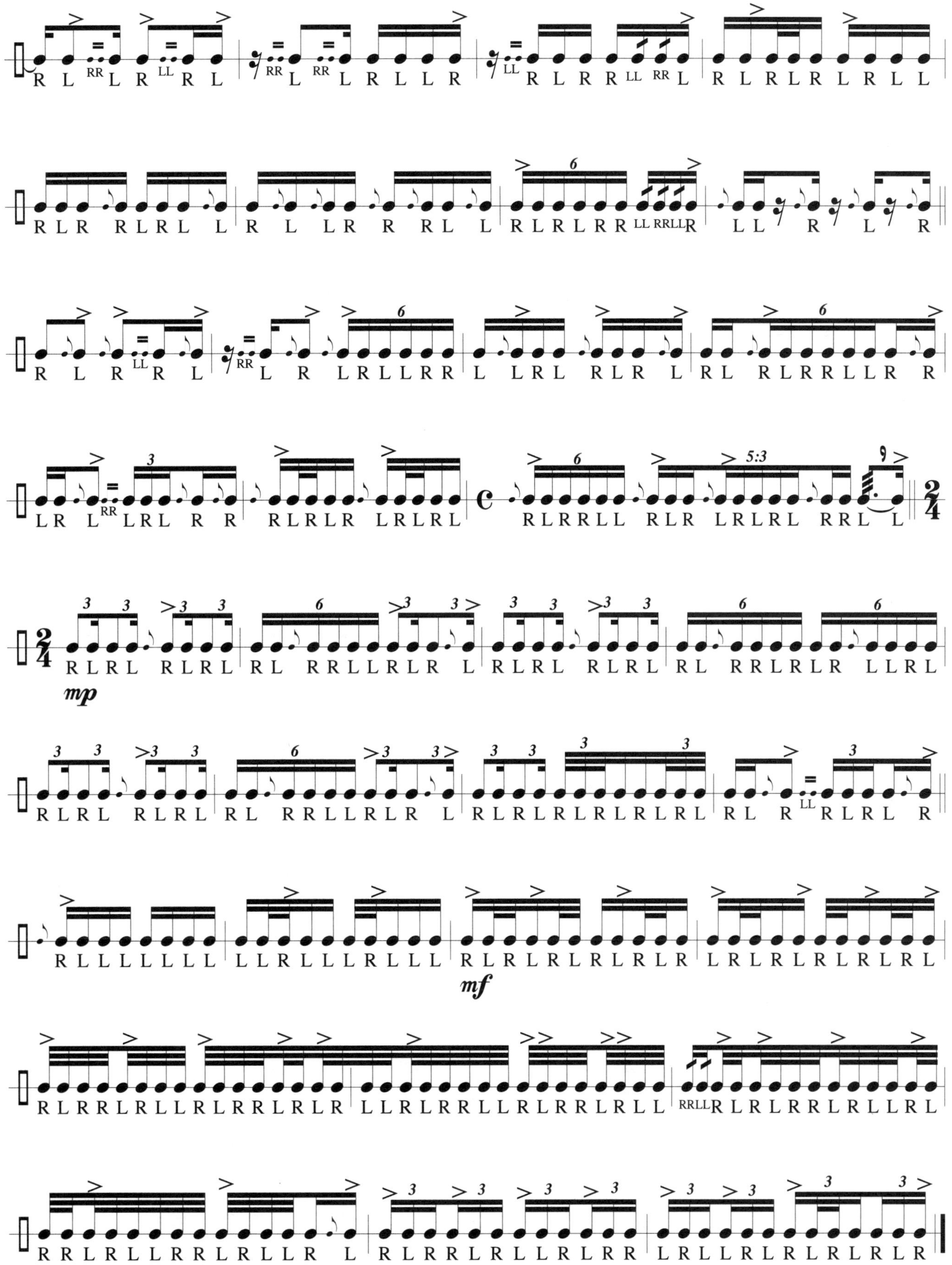
mp
mf

The Hellcats! (1998)

In 1991, I auditioned for and won a spot in the United States Military Academy Band's legendary field music group, The Hellcats. I had three great years there and performed with many outstanding musicians. This solo is dedicated to the drummers and buglers who do the sometimes unappreciated work, carrying on traditions dating back to the Revolutionary War. The drummers I had the privilege of marching with were Bob Devlin, Art Himmelberger, Warren Howe, Dana Kimble, Eric Scheffler, Don Trefethen, and John Westmacott. The first 8 bars of this solo are from *Adjutant's Call*, which can be heard on the parade field during any review at West Point. Lines 7 and 8 are a variation on the drum solo in the ever popular *Official West Point March*.

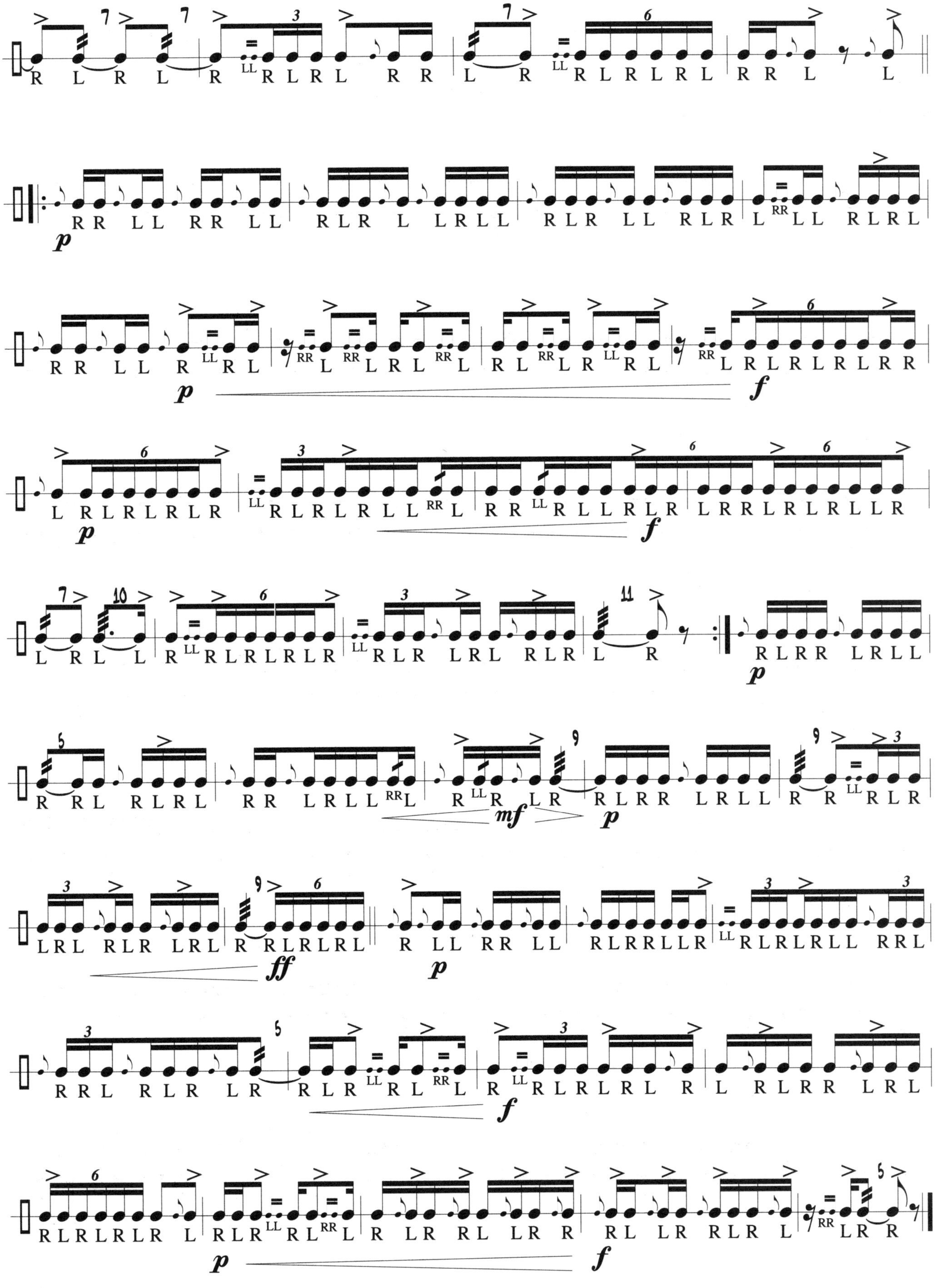

Hang Five (1999)

In 1994 I decided to leave the band at West Point and pursue my masters degree at Northwestern State University in Natchitoches, Louisiana. As luck would have it, I ended up rooming with John Brennan, a driving force behind the Cavaliers Drum & Bugle Corps.

For the next few years, we picked each others drumming minds, and I now see things in a new light. This solo utilizes some ideas he turned me on to and is dedicated to my good friend.

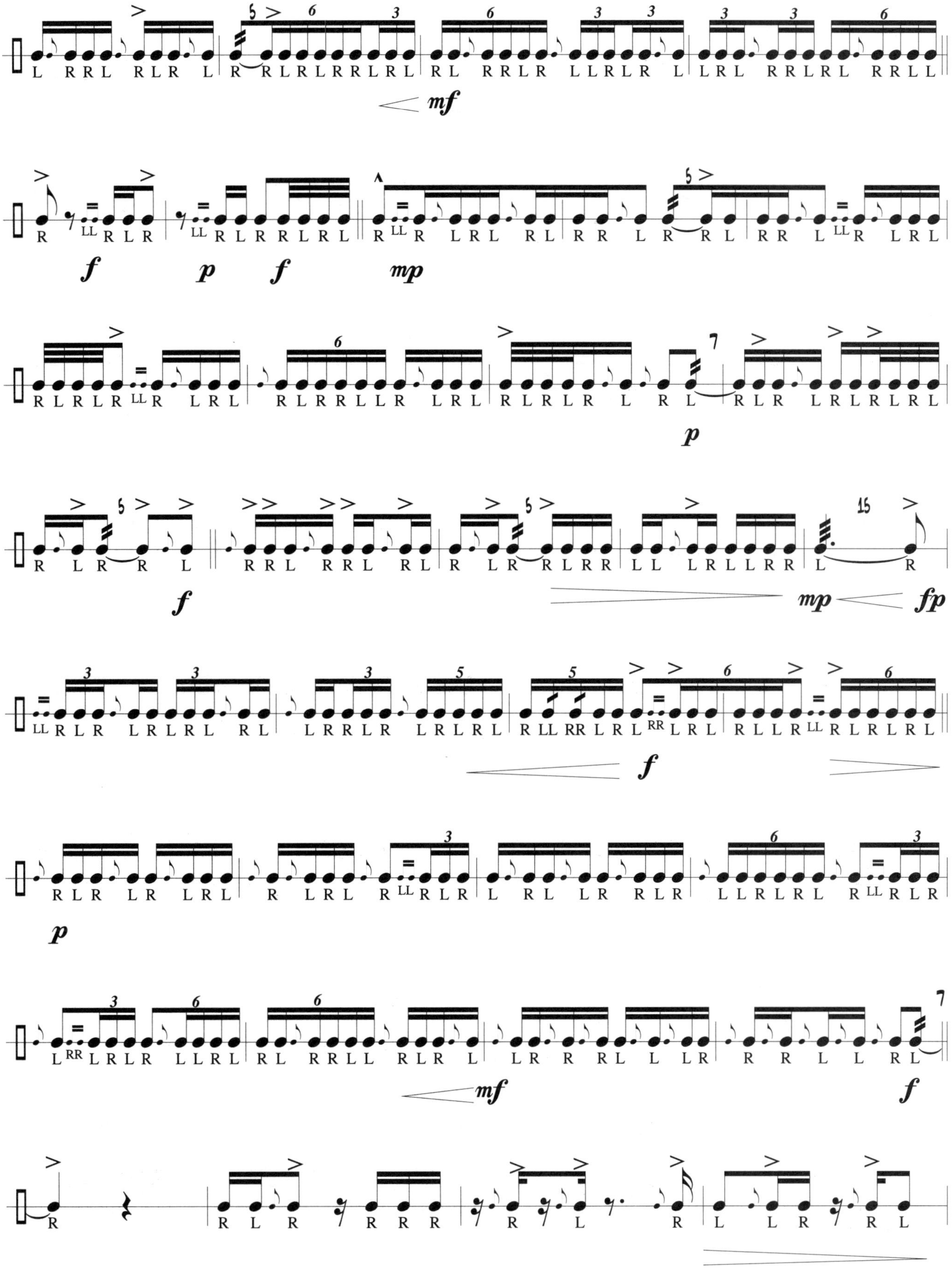
mf
f p f mp
p
f mp fp
f
p
mf f

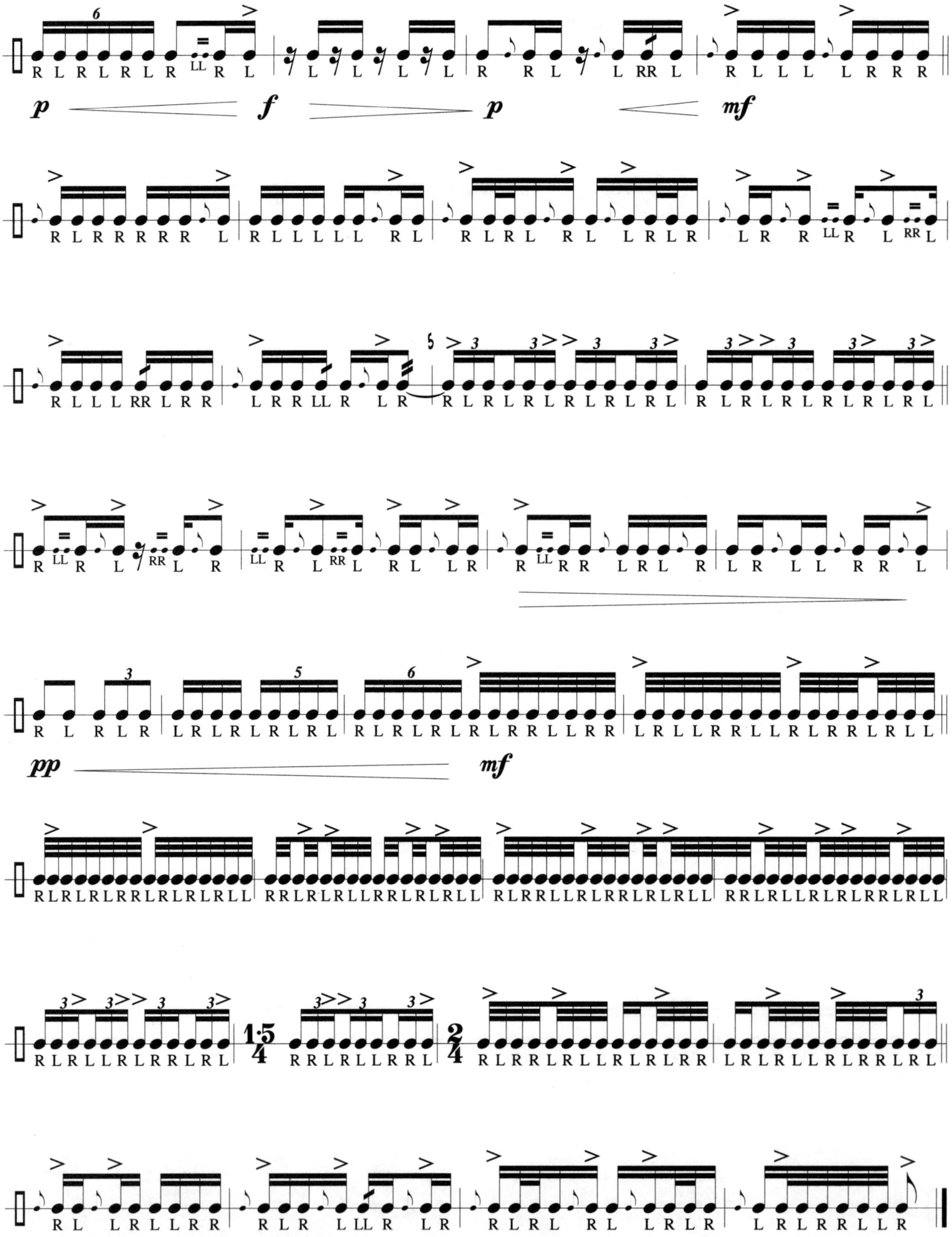
p f p mf
pp mf

The Next Generation (2001)

Through the years I have had the opportunity to teach, drum with and become friends with many talented individuals from the Young Colonials. Josh Dukes and Mark Reilly are two of the best, performing professionally as members of the United States Army's 3rd Infantry's Old Guard Fife & Drum Corps stationed at Fort Myer, Virginia. They both came into the corps during my final years as drum instructor/director and after my departure proceeded to lead the corps to its fifth Northeastern Championship in 7 years.

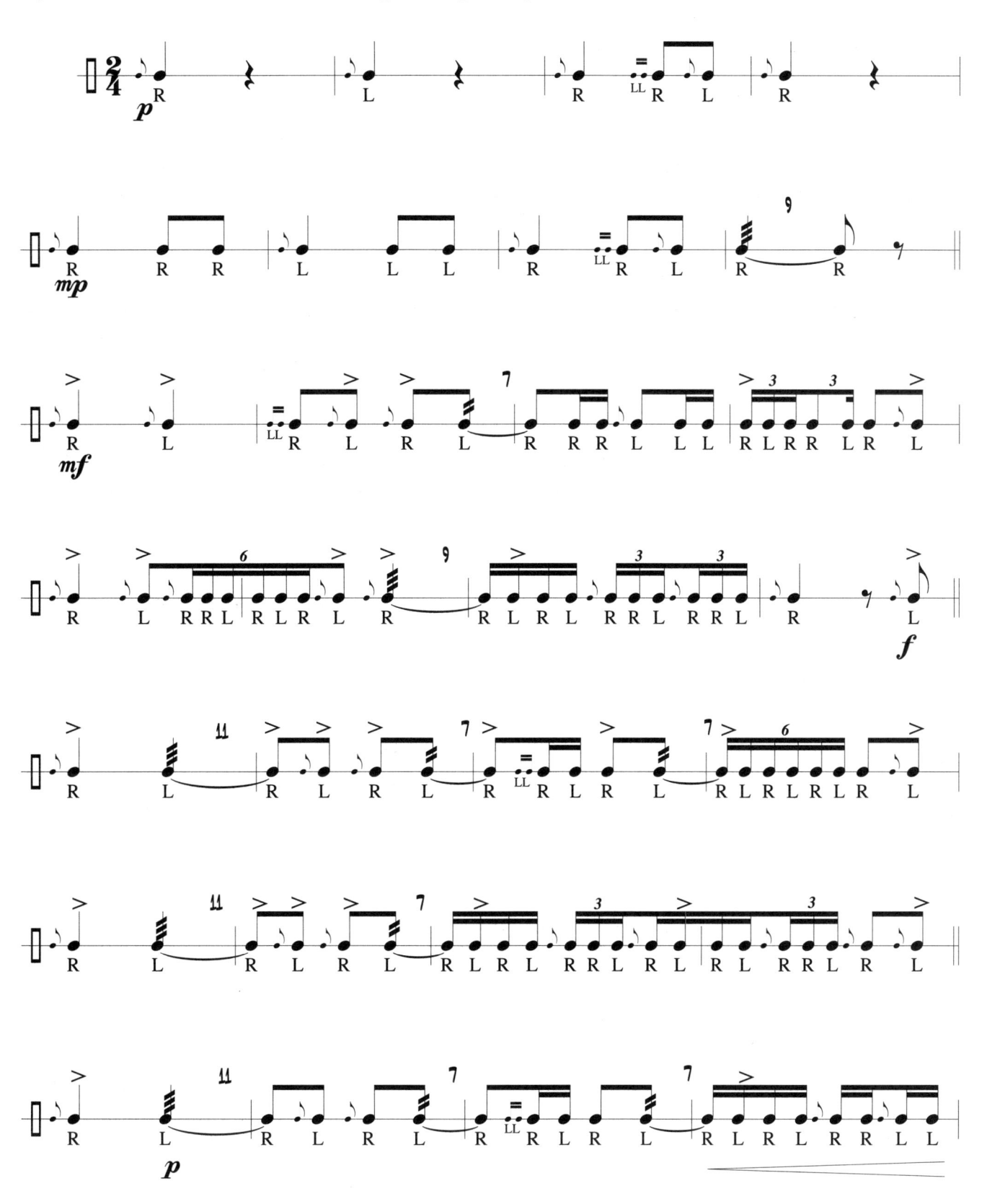

R L R L R L L R L R L R L R L R L R L R R L R L R L R R L
f
R R R L L L R L R L R L R L R L R R L L R L R L L R R L R L R
fp mf
R R R L L L R LL R L R L RR L R L R L RR L R L R R L L R L
p
R LL R R L RR L L R LL R L L RR L R R L R R L L R R L R L R L L R R L L R L
f
R LL R L R L RR L R L R R L R L R L L R L R L R R L R L R L L R L R L R L R L R L
p f
R L R L R L R LL R L R L R L R L R L R L R
p f
R L R L R L R L R L R R L R L R L R R L R L
p mf
R LL R R L R R L R R L R L R R L R R L R L R LL R L RR L
R LL R L R L R R L R L R L R R L R R L R R L R L L R L R L
p mf

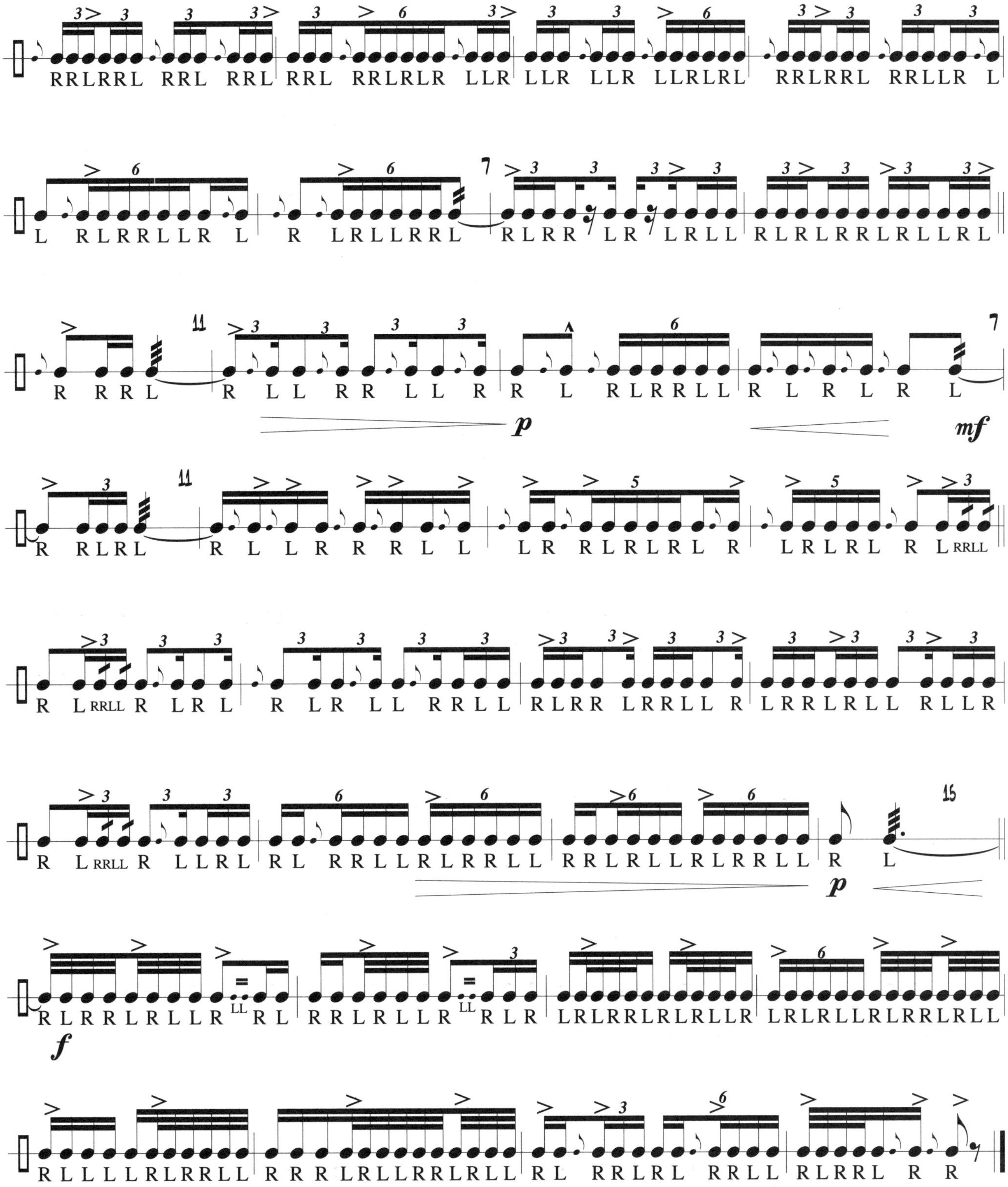
RRLRRL RRL RRL RRL RRLRLR LLR LLR LLR LLRLRL RRLRRL RRLLR L
L RLRRLLR L R LRLLRRL RLRR LR LRLL RLRLRRLRLLRL
7
R RRL R LL RR LL R R L RLRRLL R L R L R L
11 7
p mf
R RLRL R L L R R R L L LR RLRLRL R LRLRL R L RRLL
11
R L RRLL R LRL R LR LL RRLL RLRR LRRLL R LRRLRLL RLLR
R L RRLL R LLRL RL RRLLRLRRLL RRLRLLRLRRLL R L
15
p
RLRRLRLLR LL RL RRLRLLR LL RLR LRLRRLRLRLLR LRLRLLRLRRLRLL
f
RLLLLRLRRLL RRRLRLLRRLRLL RL RRLRL RRLL RLRRL R R

My Friend Jack (2001)

Growing up in the Hudson Valley, the legend of John S. Pratt (a/k/a "Jack") was never far away. In High School I played his solos. From 1991–1994 I marched in his footsteps as a member of West Point's "Hellcats," and at a muster hosted by the Civil War Troopers, I met and became friends with him. The above title is based on the ever popular *My Friend Norman* which was the required "Pratt solo" I had to perform as part of my audition into The Hellcats. Although my contributions are minute in his shadow, I'd like to dedicate this solo to him as a thank-you for all he has meant to me and the infinite number of drummers who have been influenced by him.

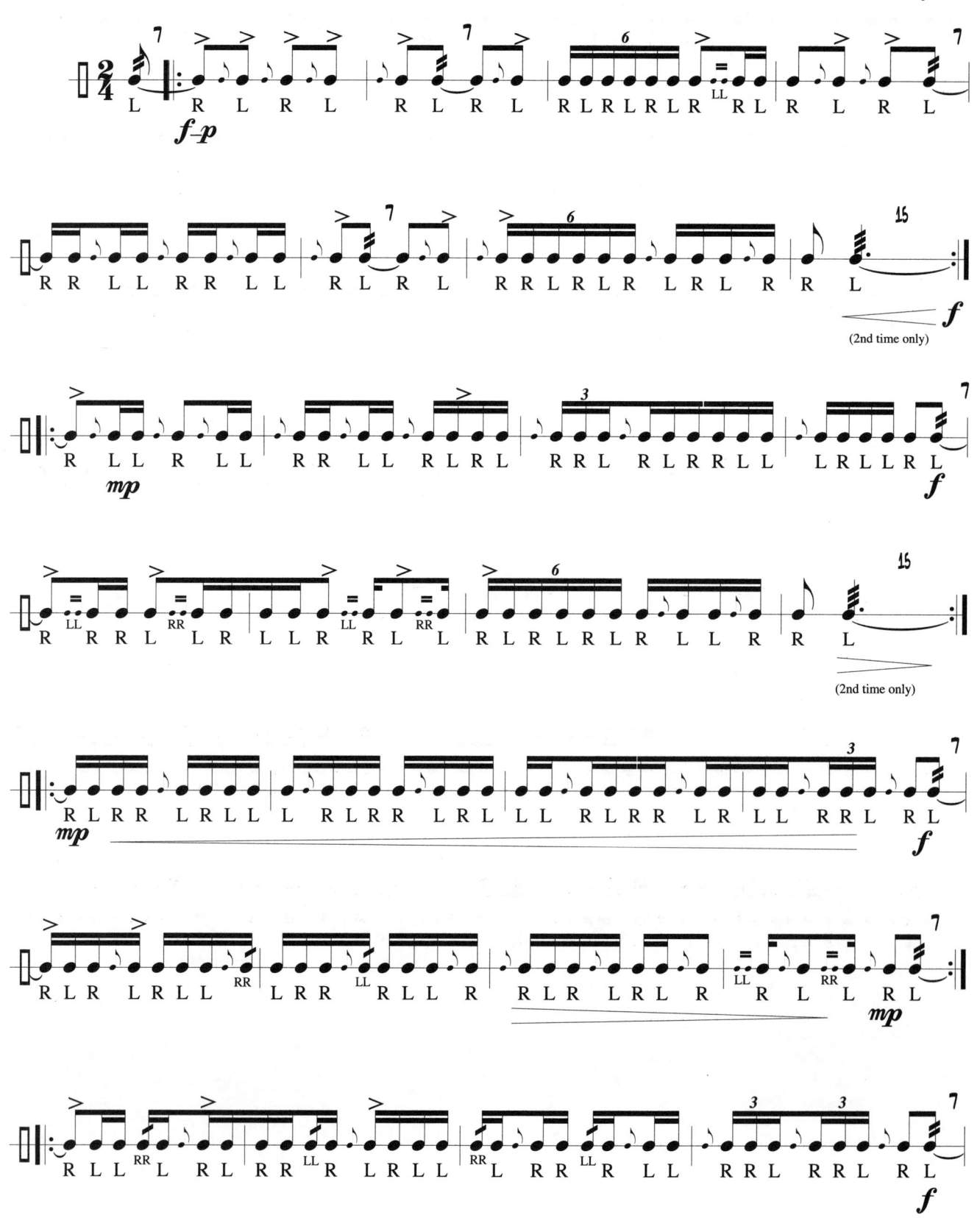

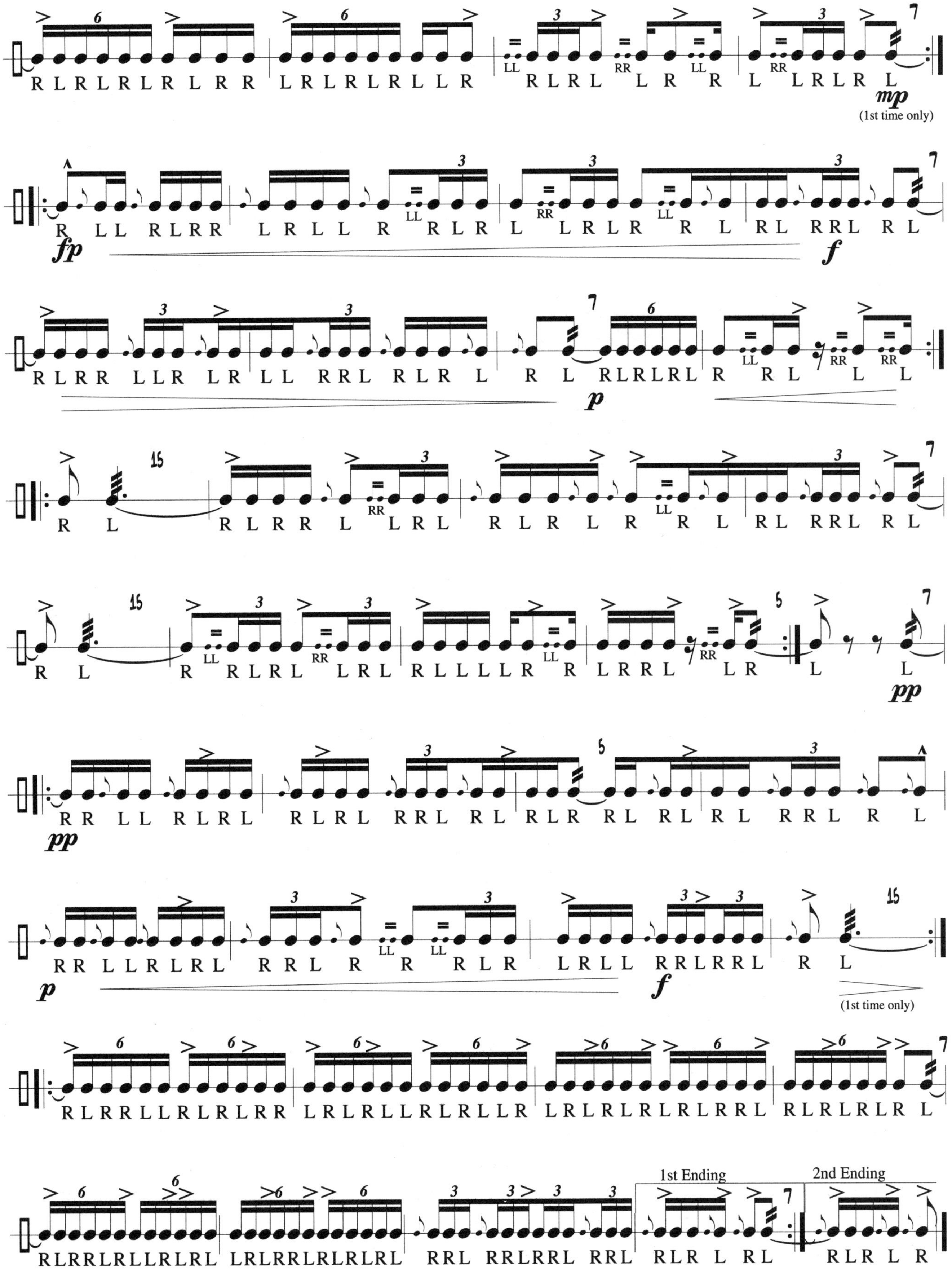
R L R L R L R L R R L R L R L R L L R LL R L R L RR L R LL R L RR L R L R L
mp
(1st time only)
R L L R L R R L R L L R LL R L R L RR L R L R LL R L R L R R L R L
fp
f
R L R R L L R L R L L R R L R L R L R L R L R L R L R LL R L RR L RR L
p
R L R L R R L RR L R L R L R L R LL R L R L R R L R L
R L R LL R L R L RR L R L R L L L L R LL R L R R L RR L R L L
pp
R R L L R L R L R L R L R R L R L R L R R L R L R L R L R R L R L
pp
R R L L R L R L R R L R LL R LL R L R L R L L R R L R R L R L
p
f
(1st time only)
R L R R L L R L R L R R L R L R L L R L R L L R L R L R L R R L R L R L R L R L R L R L R L
RLRRLRLLRLRL LRLRRLRLRLRL RRL RRLRRL RRL
1st Ending
RLR L RL
2nd Ending
RLR L R

About the Composer

Dominick Cuccia's drumming career began in October of 1976 when he joined the Young Colonials Fife & Drum Corps in Lake Carmel, New York. His instructors were Gary Gillotti and Mary Comer, both students of the Earl Sturtze method of drumming. He became drum instructor in 1981 at the age of 13, a position he held until 1994. From 1989 through 1992 the corps dominated, winning 4 consecutive Northeastern and New York State Championships, as well as many titles in the Connecticut, Hudson Valley, and Greater Danbury Area Drum Corps Associations. They also won many High Drum awards, including three Earl Sturtze trophies.

During his high school years, Dominick studied privately with Jeffrey P. Funnell. In 1985 he attended Wilkes College (now University), where he studied percussion with Robert A. Nowak. He graduated in 1990 with a bachelor's degree in music education. In 1996 he received his master's degree from Northwestern State University (NSU) of Louisiana in Natchitoches, under the direction of Ken Green. Upon graduation, Dominick was hired back at NSU, teaching major and minor study lessons, drumline, and percussion ensemble.

From 1991–1994 Dominick played with the United States Military Academy Band's legendary field music group, The Hellcats, stationed at West Point, New York. During this time he teamed up with Paul Murtha writing marching band charts for CPP Belwin. In 1997 and 1998 he performed with Walt Disney World's Founders of Freedom Fife & Drum Corps in Orlando, Florida. He also has had the opportunity to study privately with rudimental master Nick Attanasio and jazz legend Joe Morello.

In 1998 he returned to New York to pursue a career in music education and marry his drum corps sweetheart, Therese Rock (they met as members of the Young Colonials). Today he works for the Paul Effman Music Service as an instrumental teacher for children in parochial schools. In addition he serves as musical director of the Civil War Troopers Fife & Drum Corps and is a drum instructor for The Regulators Fife & Drum Corps.

In 2002 he performed at the Percussive Arts Society International Convention as part of the historic Drummers Heritage Concert and was a clinician at PASIC 2003. He is also the chairman of the music committee for The Company of Fifers & Drummers, and is music editor for the *Ancient Times,* the premier publication of the fife & drum world. His newest project, Dreaded Drummer Productions, is dedicated to preserving and advancing fife & drum music through clinics, recitals, concerts, recordings, and publications.